Cajun Music
AND Zydeco

Cajun Music
AND Zydeco

PHOTOGRAPHS BY
Philip Gould

WITH AN INTRODUCTION BY
Barry Jean Ancelet

LOUISIANA STATE UNIVERSITY PRESS   BATON ROUGE AND LONDON

For Judith, Colin, and Daniel

Many thanks to all the Cajun and zydeco musicians photographed for this book, and to their fans and families—especially their spouses—who were most gracious with their hospitality and patience.

Designer: Laura Roubique Gleason
Typeface: Janson Text
Type output: Kontrol Prepress
Printer and binder: Dai Nippon Printing Co., Ltd.

LIBRARY OF CONGRESS CATALOGING-IN-PUBLICATION DATA

Gould, Philip, 1951–
    Cajun Music and zydeco / photographs by Philip Gould ; with an
    introduction by Barry Jean Ancelet.
        p.   cm.
      ISBN 0-8071-1769-2 (alk. paper)
      ISBN 0-8071-1818-4 (spec. ed.)
      1. Musicians, Cajun—Louisiana—Portraits.   2. Zydeco musicians—
    Louisiana—Portraits.   I. Title.
    ML87.G78   1992
    781.62'410763—dc20   91-44353
                                                                                    CIP
                                                                                    MN

"Réveille" © Zachary Richard, Les Editions du Marais Bouleur/Socan, from
Bayou des Mystères, R. Z. Records 1017; all rights reserved, used by permission.
"Disco et fais do-do" © Bruce Daigrepont, Bayou Pon Pon/ASCAP, from *Stir
Up the Roux*, Rounder 6016; all rights reserved, used by permission.

Frontispiece: Clifton Chenier, last Louisiana appearance, Zydeco Festival,
Plaisance, Louisiana, 1987.

CONTENTS

PREFACE

The timing, although purely accidental, could not have been more fortunate. In March, 1974, I first came to Louisiana, taking a job as a newspaper photographer in New Iberia. I was a very green, twenty-two-year-old photojournalism graduate from San Jose State University in California. Louisiana was brand new to me and very different from the Golden State. I was still trying to get my bearings in this new-found-land when, within two weeks of arriving, I was assigned to cover the first Tribute to Cajun Music, held at the University of Southwestern Louisiana's Blackham Coliseum in Lafayette. I barely knew what or whom I was photographing there, yet I sensed the musical energy and tried—albeit somewhat blindly—to capture it on film.

Many folklorists and cultural observers mark that evening as a milepost in Cajun music's and zydeco's modern era and cultural renaissance. It was the first time in Louisiana that the music was taken out of homes and dance halls and put in a concert setting. A fierce storm wasn't enough to keep Cajuns and black Creoles from filling the arena to see many of the great legends—Nathan Abshire, Clifton Chenier, the Balfa Brothers, "Bois-sec" Ardoin, Canray Fontenot, Marc Savoy, and Dennis McGee, among others.

What occurred that night has since snowballed into a movement. Cajun music and zydeco have grown in stature and acceptance to such a degree that today they sit at the head table of American folk music, basking in a double glow of traditional integrity and commercial success. Many musicians have achieved fame and prosperity performing across the country and the world. The musical expression of a culture that many feared lost is now vibrant.

That evening eighteen years ago was the beginning of a journey for me as well. Since then I have spent most of my working life documenting as a photojournalist the cultures of Louisiana. Much of that effort has centered on Cajun music and zydeco, although not until recently as a formal project. Over the years I have carried cameras to innumerable music festivals, live radio broadcasts, and dance halls, have witnessed the traditional apprenticeship process of the young learning from their parents or other musical masters, and have become friends with many musicians and lovers of Cajun music and zydeco. I also have made south Louisiana home.

This book, *Cajun Music and Zydeco*, is a compilation of work done mostly in the last ten years. It is not encyclopedic, nor could a volume such as this ever be. Trying to photograph every Cajun and zydeco musician, festival, dance hall, and dancer would be like trying to photograph every last cowboy in the West.

Some of my greatest pleasures during the project come from the simplest moments. One of the most satisfying experiences didn't involve any musician. The scene I photographed shows two signs. One is a professionally done billboard leading to the site of the Zydeco Festival in Plaisance. The other is a simple hand-painted piece of plywood advertising "Snapp Bean for Sale." Both signs have arrows pointing the same direction, and together they make an eloquent roadside reminder that zydeco and the snap beans (*les haricots*) from which some believe the name arises still share the same cultural landscape.

My slide files also provided many poignant surprises. While searching for images for the project, I came upon one shot of a young boy intently staring, with fierce dark eyes, at the stage. One couldn't see the musician he was observing, but one could tell the boy was taking in every note and every technique. The revelation came when I realized that the boy was Steve Riley, now one of Cajun music's premier accordionists. That I should photograph, several years later, another young boy gazing up at the adult Steve Riley as he played attests the continuity of the tradition.

I have two goals in this book. The first is to portray contemporary Cajun music and zydeco as they have evolved since the first Tribute to Cajun Music in 1974. Besides being a turning point for both musics, that festival was significant for both Barry Ancelet and me. It got our feet wet. It may also have been my first real "taste of bayou water," a local phrase used in describing outsiders who seem to be staying.

My second goal is to provide readers with a visual sense of Cajun and zydeco's musical energy. I hope viewing the book will be a bit like going to a dance. Imagine a remote club nestled in a rural community that is barely on the map, where upon entering through worn screen doors one feels the flow of air from the wall-sized floor fans working hard to relieve the sultriness. Folks of all ages glide across a worn wooden dance floor as a Cajun or zydeco band belts out spirited two-steps and waltzes about lost love, death, and prison. After the last song the dancers all feel pleasantly tired, but they are still smiling, charged up and ready for at least one more. After the last photograph, I hope the reader will feel the same way.

INTRODUCTION

Barry Jean Ancelet

Cajun music and zydeco are cultural hybrids, the results of the rich blend of French, Spanish, German, Anglo-American, African, and Native American cultures that found themselves living together in south Louisiana. Basically, Cajun music is the traditional music of the white Cajuns and zydeco is the music of the black Creoles. Historically, Cajun music developed from the sounds that the French settlers took with them to the Acadian colony in the seventeenth century. Story songs called *ballades* and *complaintes* helped to filled the otherwise long and lonely nights on the edge of European civilization. Eventually, lyrics of old songs were adapted and new songs were composed to reflect new experiences. Despite long periods during which fine instruments were not available on the rugged frontier, dance tunes were preserved by whistlers and hummers and musicians with homemade versions of fiddles and flutes. The music of the early Acadians was also influenced by their new neighbors, the native Micmac Indians and the English-Scottish families who soon settled on the Acadian peninsula, which the British also claimed as Nova Scotia.

In 1755 the Acadians were arrested by the local British authorities and exiled from their homeland. Most were scattered in the American colonies. Others were sent to England or France. Although many eventually made their way back to Nova Scotia, a few thousand Acadians gravitated to Louisiana, established as a French colony in 1699. There they hoped to reestablish themselves as an Acadian society. By the time many of them arrived, Spain had acquired Louisiana from France, but Spanish administrators, eager to populate their new colony, welcomed the Acadians, who soon found themselves living alongside German Creoles, French Creoles, and Spanish Creoles, as well as Native American tribes such as the Chitimachas and the Houmas, and a few Anglo-Americans who had moved westward from the Atlantic Coast. There were also the black Creoles, descendants of the Africans brought to Louisiana by force. Most were still slaves; others had become *gens de couleur libres*—free persons of color (the phrase implied mixed blood; *nègres libres* were free persons of pure African ancestry). Some of these even owned their own slaves. The word *Creole* distinguished these French-speaking slaves and former slaves alike from their English-speaking counterparts in other parts of the South.

These various groups combined in a south Louisiana version of the American melting pot to produce what we now call Cajun and Creole cultures, each with its own music. The two major elements in this cultural gumbo were imports from France and Africa. The French tradition shared by French Creoles and Acadians served as a base for Cajun music and gave a language and specific lyrics to zydeco. The African tradition of the black Creoles served as a base for zydeco and gave rhythm, syncopation, and improvisation to Cajun music. The Native Americans contributed a wailing, terraced singing style and a drumming tradition that overlapped with black Creole origins. The Spanish contributed the guitar and a few melodies. The Germans eventually contributed the diatonic accordion, in the nineteenth century when merchants began importing the newly invented instruments from the old country. The Anglo-Americans brought lyrics that were translated into French, and jigs and reels that were adopted and adapted as tunes. Musicians from the Cajun and black Creole communities performed together and learned from each other over the years; the language of this cultural fusion was French.

By the beginning of the twentieth century, the foundations of what we now call Cajun music and zydeco were firmly in place. Ironically, the turn of the century also brought hard pressures to bear on both cultures. The Cajuns and black Creoles almost lost themselves in the Americanization process that began in earnest with World War I and the concomitant nationalistic fervor, which turned linguistic and cultural conformity into an issue of patriotism and loyalty. The development of the oil industry led people off the land and into town for new, salaried jobs that compared favorably with farming in terms of income (although miserably compared with the profits of the developers) and that gave a whole class of people a money-based economy just in time for them to be poor during the Great Depression. Schools provided the harshest lesson of all. Education became indoctrination as, in a well-intentioned but in retrospect unenlightened effort to teach them English, Cajun and Creole children were punished for speaking French in the classroom or even on the schoolgrounds. Radio and, later, television confirmed the language and economics of the American Dream. The Jim Crow segregation that followed Reconstruction had long pitted Cajuns and black Creoles, two former cultural allies, against each other in competition for the second-to-last rung on the social ladder. Now the civil rights struggle intensified problems as Cajuns and black Creoles alike jettisoned elements of their ethnicity and culture to improve their standing within their respective races.

The result of this social upheaval can be heard clearly in the Cajun music and zydeco recorded during this century. The first commercial recordings, between 1928 and 1934, include what could be called the core repertoire of Cajun music. Typically, Cajun music featured twin fiddles, or an accordion and a fiddle, accompanied by a guitar (played almost as a percussion instrument), and a triangle or spoons. The sound was tense and emotional, with an unabashedly homemade quality. Fiddlers bore down hard with their bows to be heard in the noisy dance halls. Accordions, with their four separate reed banks, were naturally louder and soon dominated the sound of Cajun music. Singers strained at the high end of their vocal ranges. Lyrics were in French and typically told of love lost and hard times. Basically, this was French blues. Songs reflected the diversity of their ancestry. In his "Valse du vacher" ("Cowboy's Waltz"), for example, a Cajun fiddler named Dennis McGee lamented the loneliness of a cowboy's life in French and to the tune of an Old World mazurka clearly influenced by the blues and Native American singing style.

By the late 1930s, Cajun music had begun to show the signs of social change. Traditional tunes were abandoned for songs borrowed from western swing and country styles. The once-dominant accordion was no longer heard in commercial recordings. Much of the tension disappeared from fiddlers' bow work and singers' delivery as bands acquired microphones and electric amplification systems. Singers even began recording songs in English, the clearest sign of all that Cajun culture was ailing.

Meanwhile, black Creole culture, brilliantly represented by Amédé Ardoin's recordings between 1928 and 1934, was otherwise virtually ignored. Some black Creoles began making blues record-

Nathan Abshire and band, first Tribute to Cajun Music, Lafayette, Louisiana, 1974

ings in English, but black French music was not recorded again commercially until the 1950s, when Boozoo Chavis and Clifton Chenier emerged with what we now call "zydeco." The clues to the origins of zydeco are the field recordings made by folklorists John and Alan Lomax for the Library of Congress between 1934 and 1937. In these recordings, groups of black Creole singers can be heard performing what were called *jurés* (from the French for "testify"), essentially Louisiana French shouts accompanied only by improvised percussion (clapping hands, stamping feet, spoons rubbed on corrugated washboards) and vocal counterpoints. Some of these songs include the first known recordings of the expression "les haricots sont pas salés" (the snap beans ain't salty), which is thought, through a fusion of sounds from the first two words, to have given zydeco its name. Later, black Creole musicians, most notably Clifton Chenier, transformed the *juré* tradition into full-blown dance music, stepping up to a chromatic piano accordion and adding elements from the blues, rock, and swing. Nevertheless, the essence of real zydeco remained firmly rooted in the highly percussive *juré* style, which was never commercially recorded.

Even though Cajun and black Creole music were not considered commercially viable in the 1940s, they did not die. They were not part of the two cultures' public fronts, but both continued to be performed at house dances and local festivities. They were available later when both cultures sought to regenerate themselves. After World War II, local record companies such as Swallow Records in Ville Platte took up the slack left when national labels stopped recording regional music. Cajun music and zydeco reclaimed their places on the public record. They were not, however, universally appreciated even within the region. Some upwardly mobile Cajuns and black Creoles had learned to be ashamed of such rough displays of tradition. Nevertheless, every week in the dance halls, musicians provided sounds that reminded Cajuns and Creoles that they weren't just like everybody else, that there might be something worth preserving here. Some, such as Iry Lejeune, Nathan Abshire, Lawrence Walker, Aldus Roger, Belton Richard, Clifton Chenier, and Boozoo Chavis, are well known and celebrated as heroes. Others, such as Evril Menard, Varise Conner, Freeman Fontenot, and Sidney Babineaux, are less famous, but no less important. They all helped to bring us through the hard times to the renaissance covered by Philip Gould in this book.

Today Cajun music and zydeco continue to be closely related, sharing many stylistic elements and much of their repertoire, but they are also distinct, each the pride and joy of its cultural parents. Both are bluesy, improvisational dance music. Yet even when playing the same song, musicians from the two styles follow their own cultural imperatives. Cajun music tends to be smoother and more lilting than zydeco, which leans toward a highly percussive and syncopated sound. There seems to be a rule among Cajun musicians that the real stuff must be in French; zydeco singers do not hesitate to use English lyrics, although they rarely fail to include a few French songs in each performance.

The fact that these two musical cousins are still around and determining their own way is somewhat remarkable, considering that both supposedly have been "dying" for at least fifty years. In typical contrary south Louisiana fashion, neither has. Underlying this book about the people and places on the cultural landscape of Cajun music and zydeco is the story of how these musics not only survived, but even thrived. The story begins during a critical transitional period in the mid-1970s, when a festival helped to proclaim what became known as the Louisiana French renaissance movement—and when, coincidentally, I first met Philip Gould.

The date was March 26, 1974. The occasion was the first Tribute to Cajun Music festival in Lafayette. Philip, as I recall, had just arrived from California to take a job as staff photographer at the *Daily Iberian*. The festival was one of his first assignments. What an introduction to the area! More than twelve thousand people had gathered to celebrate music that was widely dismissed, even by some Cajuns, as "nothing but chanky-chank." The moment proved to be a pivotal one in the effort to revitalize Louisiana's French culture and language. Philip didn't know much about what he was shooting, but he realized that it was important. We who had organized the festival knew a little more, but even we were amazed at what happened. The event turned into a mass rally, but instead of politicians and ideologues, it was musicians who took the stage to express a subtle but powerful message of cultural pride. Over the years we all have come to understand more about the phenomenon of that stormy night and what has happened since.

The idea of a festival honoring Cajun and Creole music was conceived in 1973. My own involvement in the project came as a result of a personal exile experience in France. Toward the end of what seemed to be an interminable academic year there, I was feeling out of place and I didn't understand why. I spoke the language fluently—although my French friends often interrupted our conversations to comment on how cute my accent and expressions were. I had studied French culture and civilization for four years in high school and three years in college, so I was familiar with the place and the people even before I arrived. Yet I was homesick. Something was missing and I didn't know what or why.

One afternoon while walking back from the marketplace in Nice, I saw a poster announcing "Roger Mason joue la musique de la Louisiane" (Roger Mason plays music from Louisiana). I was curious and decided to see what this was all about. The evening of the concert, I arrived just in time to hear the strains of "The Crowley Two-step" drift up from the basement where Mason was performing. The music washed over me like a warm tide. This was what was missing. Like the rest of my generation, I had grown up on rock and roll, but I had heard Cajun music on local television on Saturday afternoons when the choice was between that and golf, and on the record player during barbecues or crawfish boils when Daddy got to choose the records. It was something that we all heard, but rarely really listened to. That night, Cajun music was the most comforting sound I had heard in a year.

After the performance I headed backstage to tell Mason what his music had done for me. I learned that he was an American air force brat who spoke French fluently, having grown up in Europe. In no way a Cajun himself, he had encountered Cajun music through the American folk music revival movement and had fallen in love with it. Living now in Paris, he had discovered that the French enjoyed this profoundly American folk music with lyrics they could understand, and he was making a modest living playing it on the coffeehouse circuit throughout France. I told him I was from south Louisiana myself and that the evening had chased away my blues. "Oh, so you're from Cajun country," he said. "Then you must know all the great people I learned from: Dewey Balfa, Nathan Abshire . . ." I didn't know any of them, and it occurred to me that something was wrong. I knew about the châteaux along the Loire in France, but virtually nothing about the cultures along the Bayou Teche in my native state. I knew about French artists and authors and wines and cheeses from books, yet I had grown up and lived all my life in south Louisiana and didn't know anything about the Cajun musicians whom this American in Paris considered heroes. "If you want to know something about all this," Mason suggested with a grin, "talk to Dewey Balfa. He lives near Basile, Louisiana."

When I returned home a couple of months later, I immediately borrowed my father's pickup truck, drove to Basile, got directions to

Dewey Balfa's house, and knocked on his door. When he answered I blurted out: "Mr. Balfa? My name is Barry Ancelet, from Lafayette, and I need to know who you are." Dewey was obviously puzzled. When I told him about my evening with Roger Mason, he laughed and invited me in. He immediately accepted me as a sort of cultural godchild and began filling in the gaps in my formal education.

One of the first things Dewey suggested was that I start a collection project. He had worked with Ralph Rinzler (a folklorist with the Newport Folk Festival in the 1960s and the Smithsonian Institution since 1967) and had learned much about his own culture by considering the questions Rinzler asked. Several folklorists had made field recordings in south Louisiana, including John and Alan Lomax in the 1930s, Bill Owens in the 1940s, Harry Oster in the 1950s, and Rinzler in the 1960s, but no one had found a place to leave copies of any of these collections within the state. Dewey reasoned that we ought to develop our own information bank. When I protested that I didn't have that kind of money, he countered: "You have enough for one reel of tape? Buy it and record. When it's full, buy another one. When it's full, you'll have two, and that's the beginning of a collection." Embarrassed by the brutal simplicity of his logic, I went straightway to the electronics store. In January, 1974, I began my "collection," recording stories and songs with Barbara Ryder, who was majoring in French at Colby College in Maine.

Toward the end of 1973, Dewey had attended an informal meeting with James Domengeaux, founder and chairman of the Council for the Development of French in Louisiana (CODOFIL). Dewey had been warned that although Domengeaux was fighting passionately for the survival of the French language in Louisiana, he saw no value in Cajun music, and not to bring up the subject. But when Dewey was introduced, Domengeaux recognized the name and asked if he was one of those Balfa brothers who were playing Cajun music at folk festivals around the country. Since Domengeaux had opened the door, Dewey decided to walk in. Admitting that he was indeed one of those Balfas, he went on to say that he had been one of the first Cajun musicians to perform at the Newport Folk Festival, in 1964, and that he had seen how powerful Cajun music could be in such a setting; he insisted that Cajun music could galvanize the still-struggling Louisiana French movement. "You've got the power," Dewey dared. "If you put on a festival here, you'll see what the music can do for our people." Domengeaux let the conversation drift away from this uncomfortable track, but the seed had been sown.

Balfa and Domengeaux met again at the invitation of two National Endowment for the Arts fieldworkers, Ron and Fay Stanford, who wanted to establish a folklore program and were exploring ways to take advantage of a visit by Rinzler and the eminent French ethnomusicologist Claudie Marcel-Dubois. They thought that as a state agency established to preserve the French language and culture in Louisiana, CODOFIL might be a likely sponsor. By then Domengeaux had begun to agree that language does not exist in a vacuum. Although he did not have a place for a folklore program in CODOFIL, he suggested that the University of Southwestern Louisiana, in Lafayette, might. He was also interested in the visit of so renowned a French scholar as Marcel-Dubois. CODOFIL had agreed to host an international convention of French-speaking journalists in March, 1974, and Domengeaux was looking for newsworthy events for them to cover. I was working as a student aide at CODOFIL while waiting to graduate in May, 1974, and Domengeaux invited me to attend a convention meeting. Dewey and I resuscitated the idea of a music festival and suggested that such an event might capture the attention of the visiting journalists. We also suggested that the visiting Rinzler and Marcel-Dubois might be most helpful in exerting a behind-the-scenes influence toward the establishment of a permanent folklore program at the university.

Varise Conner, first Tribute to Cajun Music.

Eventually, Rinzler's meeting with USL president Ray Authement spawned the creation of the Center for Acadian and Creole Folklore. CODOFIL and the French journalists, meanwhile, got a passionate display of reborn cultural pride at the first Tribute to Cajun Music. And Dewey got his experiment.

Domengeaux appointed a committee to oversee the organization of the concert. Chaired by a Mamou attorney and cultural activist, Paul Tate, the committee met several times to discuss philosophy and establish basic guidelines, but the actual planning of the event took place on a much smaller scale in the CODOFIL office. Domengeaux asked Carol Rachou, a Lafayette-based record producer, to help with arrangements, and Rachou placed his catalog of musicians at our disposal. Rachou also sent his student aide, Keith Cravey, to assist with the technical aspects of the preparations. Cravey, a hard-core pragmatist, wandered into our den of dreamers and asked about what was under way. I explained our intent to pay tribute to Cajun and Creole music in a grand concert. He listened patiently. When I finished my pitch, he looked me in the eye, said, "You're crazy," and walked out. Twenty minutes later he was back. His boss had told him that even if he thought we were crazy, his job was to help produce the tribute. "So let's get started," he said as he sat down next to a telephone and began calling for amplifiers and speakers, stages and locations; we were finally moving from philosophy to action.

As things began to fall into place, the stakes were raised. At Dewey's suggestion, Rinzler became involved in the festival's production, lending the prestige of the Smithsonian Institution to the project. He served as a programming consultant by phone and agreed to come to Lafayette to help host the concert.

We knew almost nothing about what we were so enthusiastically doing. We had no idea who might be interested in attending such an event. At first, the proposed location for our little academic exercise was the USL Student Union theater, which seats a few hundred. Then we began to receive feedback from the public, and there seemed to be more community interest than we had thought. So we upgraded our expectations and moved across the hall to the Union ballroom, which holds a thousand. Our expectations continued to grow, and we raised our sights first to Lafayette's Municipal Auditorium, with a capacity of around three thousand, then to Blackham Coliseum, with eight thousand seats. We panicked and backtracked several times along the way, but eventually decided to go for broke: we announced that the Tribute to Cajun Music would be held in Blackham Coliseum.

Domengeaux was especially nervous. Following his original plan, he had tied the event to the visit of more than 150 French-language journalists from all over the world. The concert was to showcase the vitality of Louisiana's French culture and language. But what if no one came? Or what if only a few thousand came? The coliseum would appear half empty. Many people went to weekend dances, but a concert? Cajuns were notoriously suspicious of such new affairs. And what if only older people came? That certainly would not appear vital to 150 perceptive journalists.

To make things worse, the afternoon of the concert the skies opened, dumping nearly a foot of rain on most of south Louisiana, accompanied by a spectacular display of lightning. At that point we weren't even sure that the musicians would come. After all, no one was being paid a cent, not even travel money. The concert was scheduled to start at seven-thirty. By four o'clock the sound system was set up and ready. Fiddler Lionel Leleux had arrived early, pants rolled above his knees and instrument case held high and dry. His sound check sounded great—but what if no one came? Around four-thirty a family showed up, three generations strong, and we began to feel better. Soon enough, the coliseum started to fill, mostly with the same sort of folks—whole families. To our surprise and relief, a great many people were coming—and young ones, too. And every musician showed up; we even got a few extras who were added to the program literally at the last minute.

By seven-thirty, the coliseum was not only filled, but overflowing. Every seat was taken except for the 150 chairs reserved for the journalists, on the floor directly in front of the stage. When the show didn't start right on time, the crowd correctly guessed that we were waiting for whoever was supposed to sit in those empty chairs. The journalists had been delayed by the weather and the incredible traffic jam outside the coliseum. As soon as they arrived, they were escorted to their reserved seats. The crowd, knowing the show could now begin, erupted in applause. The journalists assumed the clapping was for them and gratefully acknowledged the warm "reception." Meanwhile, several thousand people stranded outside because of the fire code limits remained under their umbrellas, asking only that the doors be left open so that they might listen. One CODOFIL official reopened the doors and let them in, reasoning that there was a worse risk outside than in. The fire marshal came to me frantic, wanting to know how this had happened. I didn't know, but I was reasonably sure he wouldn't shut us down: his father was playing in the second group.

From the outset it was obvious to everyone that this was a magic moment. We all felt it, organizers, musicians, audience, and journalists alike. Area newspapers reported on the event with a newly discovered pride. For example, the Opelousas *Daily World*, which only a few years earlier had run an editorial entitled "They Call That Music??!!" maligning Cajun music, now described the festival in glowing terms in a story headlined "Coliseum Shivers Under Impact of Music Rally."

The program was carefully designed to demonstrate, with living musicians, the history and development of Cajun music and zydeco as we understood them at the time. Ballad singers Inez Catalon and

Marcus Landry represented the oldest, unaccompanied tradition, with songs traceable all the way back to France. Twin fiddlers Dennis McGee and Sady Courville played tunes from the earliest instrumental days, before the accordion came to dominate Cajun music. Marc Savoy, Lionel Leleux, Varise Conner, and Don Montoucet reproduced the sound of early accordion-driven house-dance bands from around the turn of the century. The Balfa Brothers recapitulated the message of the whole festival, demonstrating the evolution of Cajun music with the resources of their own band. Nathan Abshire and the latest version of his often-reconstituted Pine Grove Boys performed in the style of Cajun music's revival period ushered in by Iry Lejeune following World War II. Blackie Forestier and his Cajun Aces, one of the hottest dance-hall bands at the time, provided the modern sound of Cajun music. The Ardoin Family Band, featuring Alphonse "Bois-sec" Ardoin and Canray Fontenot, demonstrated early black Creole music in the tradition of their legendary cousin, Amédé Ardoin. Clifton Chenier dazzled the crowd with his sometimes bluesy, sometimes rocking urban zydeco. And erstwhile Cajun crooner Jimmy C. Newman came home from Nashville to perform a few country-influenced classics and his then-current hit, "Lâche pas la patate," the title of which (meaning literally "Don't let go of the potato," but figuratively "Hang in there") came to serve as a motto for both the festival and the entire Louisiana French renaissance movement.

There was a spirit of elegance and formality unusual among a people famed for their informal approach to life. The evening was hosted by Rinzler and USL Hebrard Professor of French Hosea Phillips. Most in the audience who had heard Cajun music before had done so in dark, smoke-filled dance halls, paying only enough attention to know when to put the next foot down. The concert format was deliberately designed to prevent people from dancing. As they found themselves sitting and listening closely to the music for the first time, many discovered that it was actually quite beautiful. Domengeaux himself realized that he apparently had only heard Cajun music poorly performed until then, and he soon mobilized CODOFIL's state-funded forces on the cultural front, announcing that "music and language are inseparable in Louisiana."

The festival was a powerful medium. Afterward, I realized that I had understood only the second part of Dewey's message. He had said, "You'll see what the music can do for our people." We were aiming the message out to the audience. But Dewey had meant the first part, too: that we, the producers, would see. His message was aimed backstage as well, and indeed, we saw.

Another thing we saw, however, was that Louisiana French music did not seem to renewing itself. Of the musicians who performed that first year, the youngest was Marc Savoy, born in 1940, and he was an anomaly. The rest were in their fifties, sixties, seventies, and

Marc Savoy, 1974 Tribute to Cajun Music.

eighties. But as improbable as it may have seemed that night, within a very few years the situation began to change. The CODOFIL movement regenerated pride among the Cajuns in general. Its festival and others brought much positive attention to Cajun and zydeco music. Outside the area, local musicians were showered in glory at such prestigious events as the Chicago Folk Festival, the Smithsonian's Festival of American Folklife, and the National Folk Festival. Closer to home, the New Orleans Jazz and Heritage Festival added Louisiana French music to its statewide focus. Even closer, events such as the Church Point Cajun Days and the Mamou Cajun Music Festival celebrated local traditions and encouraged young musicians. Meanwhile, Dewey Balfa's Folk Artists in the Schools project, funded by the Southern Folk Revival Project, the Acadiana Arts Council, and the National Endowment for the Arts, invaded what had been hostile territory, taking the message of cultural pride into the classrooms. Soon enough, young musicians began to emerge.

Some of them first appeared at the grass-roots level in response to an ongoing effort to revive Cajun music in the countryside. Since 1965, the Newport Folk Festival Foundation, in cooperation with the Louisiana Folk Foundation, had sponsored contests and performances throughout south Louisiana to discover new talent and encourage the preservation of the tradition. By the early 1970s, these contests included categories for emerging young musicians. The roll of winners of the Church Point Cajun Days accordion contests from 1974, 1975, and 1976, for example, reads like a who's who of contemporary Cajun music: Danny Brasseaux, Paul Daigle, and Wayne Toups. About the same time, accordionist Nathan Abshire took on a class of apprentices, among them Robert Jardell. Other old masters began to get the same idea. Marc Savoy, whose music store is nicknamed "The Bunker" and whose motto is "I don't go to work; I go to war!" virtually reinvented the diatonic accordion from the inside out, building on the earlier work of craftsmen such as Sidney Brown and Shine Mouton. Savoy in turn inspired a new corps of accordion builders, whose instruments were needed to meet an ever-increasing demand.

Some musicians, rather than simply coming up in the genre, made a conscious intellectual choice to enter (or reenter) it. Michael Doucet and Zachary Richard had undergone what could be thought of as exile experiences, Doucet while a student at Louisiana State University in nearby but basically un-Cajun Baton Rouge, and Richard while on a quest to become a folk singer in New York City. Both were inspired to rediscover the language and culture of their heritage. The two knew each other from high school, and they joined forces with other young singers such as Roy Harrington and Kenneth Richard in the Bayou des Mystères Band, bringing a youthful, rock-oriented approach to performing and arranging Cajun music. At the same time, they discovered and studied the old masters. Doucet apprenticed himself to a pantheon of great Cajun and Creole fiddlers, including Dennis McGee, Dewey Balfa, Canray Fontenot, Lionel Leleux, and Varise Conner. Zachary Richard revived old ballads with crystal-clear vocals and haunting, intricate harmonies. He also apprenticed himself to the master accordionist Felix Richard.

The Bayou des Mystères Band also found eager and enthusiastic audiences in Quebec and in the Acadian community in New Brunswick and Nova Scotia. Trained in history at Tulane, Zachary Richard was especially inspired by the moving story of his own people and by the activist nature of French Canadian politics. He was among the first to compose songs that reflected both the Acadian exile and the more recent acculturation and assimilation of the Cajuns. Many of his lyrics served as miniature history lessons for a people who had never had the opportunity to learn about their own past.

Richard's compositions did not always sound like traditional dance music. He wanted Cajuns to take a break from dancing and to listen seriously. The combination of emotional Cajun music with French lyrics and contemporary rock-oriented arrangements made Richard an overnight sensation in Quebec and even in France, where he has had several huge hits and gold records.

Richard and Doucet performed at the second Tribute to Cajun Music in 1975. Their performance was laden with passion and politics and was completely misunderstood. As Richard sang his emotional complaint "Réveille" through clenched teeth, many older members of the crowd probably wondered why Eddie Richard's boy

Réveille

Réveille Réveille c'est les goddams
   qui viennent
bruler la récolte.
Réveille Réveille, hommes Acadiens,
pour sauver le village.
Mon grand grand grand grand père
est v'nu de la Bretagne,
le sang de ma famille est mouillé
   l'Acadie
et là les maudits viennent
nous chasser comme des bêtes
détruire les saintes familles
nous jeter tous au vent.

Réveille Réveille

J'ai entendu parler de monter avec
   Beausoleil
pour prendre le fusil battre les sacrés
   maudits.
J'ai entendu parler d'aller en la
   Louisiane,
pour trouver de la bonne paix
là bas dans la Louisiane.

Réveille Réveille

J'ai vu mon pauvre père
était fait prisonnier
pendant que ma mère
ma belle mère braillait.
J'ai vu ma belle maison
était mise aux flammes,
et moi j'su resté orphelin
Orphelin de l'Acadie.

Réveille Réveille c'est les goddams qui
   viennent
voler les enfants.
Réveille Réveille, hommes Acadiens,
pour sauver l'héritage.

Awaken

Awaken Awaken the goddams [British]
   are coming
to burn the crops.
Awaken Awaken, men of Acadia,
to save the town.
My great-great-great-grandfather
came from Brittany,
the blood of my family is soaked in
   Acadia
and now those damned people are
   coming
hunting us like animals,
destroying the sacred families
casting us all to the winds.

Awaken Awaken

I've heard talk of going up with
   Beausoleil
to take up arms to fight the damn
   bastards.
I've heard talk of going to Louisiana,
to find sweet peace
down there in Louisiana.

Awaken Awaken

I saw my poor father
taken prisoner
while my mother
my beautiful mother wept.
I saw my beautiful house
set afire,
and I remained an orphan
Orphan of Acadia.

Awaken Awaken the goddams are
   coming
to steal the children.
Awaken Awaken, men of Acadia,
To save the heritage.

was so mad. On the other hand, the contemporary arrangements of Richard's Bayou des Mystères Band and of Coteau, a group brought together by Doucet shortly afterward, began to attract the attention of the young hip crowds around Lafayette.

In Coteau, Doucet and another young Cajun musician, Bessyl Duhon, joined forces with rockers Bruce McDonald and Dana Breaux on electric guitars, Kenny Blevins on drums, and Gary Newman, son of Jimmy C. Newman, on bass. These eclectic resources made for a rich but volatile blend, highly original and inspired yet charged with personality clashes that threatened to blow the band apart. Before it indeed did blow apart, Coteau succeeded in attracting a young audience for its souped-up version of Cajun music. Once Coteau got them that far, many were hooked.

Coteau was Doucet's money band. When it broke up around

Zachary Richard, second Tribute to Cajun Music, Lafayette, 1975.

1976, he turned his attention to his hobby band, Beausoleil, a much more traditionally oriented group originally built around Duhon and the Richard brothers, Kenneth and Sterling. It is through Beausoleil that Doucet's influence has been most strongly felt in the Cajun community. The group accompanied the award-winning Louisiane Bien Aimée Bicentennial Exhibition on a trip to France and cut its first album, *Beausoleil la nuit*, in Paris during an all-night session at the famed Pathé-Marconi studios. Ironically, Bruce McDonald, the rocking lead guitarist from the now-defunct Coteau, accompanied Beausoleil on the trip to France. Thus, although the record has its traditional side, it also includes a hint of the wonderful creative tension that fueled Coteau, whose one live session has not been released.

Beausoleil gained momentum, earning regular slots on the Lafayette nightclub scene and an enthusiastic following among the college crowd. Doucet deftly blended rock, jazz, and classical styles into the carefully researched traditional base of the group. An expanded version of Beausoleil played at the third Tribute to Cajun Music, now moved outdoors to Girard Park, in 1976. The group's performance proved to many doubting traditionalists that young people with long hair and jeans could play Cajun music. Later that

year, during the weeks surrounding the Fourth of July, Cajun and Creole musicians were prominently featured at the Smithsonian's three-month-long bicentennial run of its annual Festival of American Folklife. This event made the national news and echoed back home to Louisiana. Now the local media were pointing to Cajun music as a source of pride, not shame.

It was beginning to appear that Cajun music had a chance of passing to at least one more generation. In January, 1977, Beausoleil was invited by the Smithsonian's Office of Folklife Programs to perform at Jimmy Carter's inaugural festivities, largely on the strength of sixteen-year-old Sterling Richard's vocals, which were clearly inspired by the legendary Iry Lejeune. Later that year at the Tribute to Cajun Music, a teenager named Marc Boudreaux joined veterans Octa Clark, Hector Duhon, and the Dixie Ramblers for a couple of songs. His energetic yet respectful performance was impressive. One member of the large audience, a young bluegrass musician named Bruce Daigrepont, whose family had moved from Avoyelles Parish to the New Orleans area, decided that he wanted to play Cajun music, too. He traded his banjo for an accordion and within a few months formed a band. Daigrepont quickly established himself as

Disco et fais do-do	Disco and Fais Do-Do
A peu près cinq ans passés, je pouvais pas espérer	About five years ago, I couldn't wait
Pour quitter la belle Louisiane.	To leave beautiful Louisiana,
Quitter ma famille, quitter mon village,	Leave my family, leave my town,
Sortir de la belle Louisiane.	Get out of beautiful Louisiana.
J'aimais pas l'accordéon, j'aimais pas le violon,	I didn't like the accordion, I didn't like the fiddle,
Je voulais pas parler le français.	I didn't want to speak French.
A cette heure, je suis ici dans la Californie.	Now I'm here in California
J'ai changé mon idée.	I've changed my mind.
Je dis, "Hé yaie yaie. Je manque la langue Cadjin.	I say, "Hey yaie yaie. I miss the Cajun language.
C'est juste en anglais parmi les Américains.	Everything's in English among the Americans.
J'ai manqué Mardi Gras. Je mange pas du gombo.	I missed Mardi Gras. I don't eat gumbo.
Et je vas au disco, mais je manque le fais do-do.	And I go to the disco, but I miss the fais do-do.
J'avais l'habitude de changer la station	I used to change the station
Quand j'entendais les chansons cadjins.	When I heard Cajun songs.
Moi, je voulais entendre la même musique,	I wanted to listen to the same music
Pareil comme les Américains.	As the rest of the Americans.
A cette heure, je m'ennuie de les vieux Cadjins.	Now I long for the old Cajuns.
C'est souvent je joue leurs disques.	I play their records often.
Et moi, je donnerais à peu près deux cents piastres	And I'd give about two hundred bucks
Pour une livre des écrevisses . . .	For a pound of crawfish . . .

an important innovator in the genre, composing new songs that soon became part of the tradition. His "Valse de la Rivière Rouge," pointing out the difference between money and happiness, struck a resonant chord among Cajuns in the throes of the depression caused by the oil bust of the 1980s. In "Two-step de Marksville," Daigrepont described the founding of his hometown, and in "Disco et fais do-do," he faced his own rebellious past and the subsequent cultural reawakening of an entire generation.

Other young Cajun musicians were similarly inspired. At the 1978 Tribute to Cajun Music, eight of the twenty-two groups invited to perform consisted entirely of musicians under the age of thirty. Two of those, Tim Broussard and the Cajun Ramblers and the black Creole Sam Brothers, consisted entirely of musicians under twenty. Their approach was distinctly nontraditional, reflecting years of influence by country, rock, blues, and soul music. Of course, earlier innovators, such as Joseph Falcon, Lawrence Walker, Aldus Roger, and Belton Richard, had initially sounded just as new and surprising.

The young troops took their places alongside the old guard on festival stages and dance-hall bandstands, and especially in the new breed of music venues—restaurants such as Mulate's, Préjean's, Bélizaire's, and Randol's, where one does not have to be of legal drinking age to hear the music, and where children can learn to dance from their grandparents. In later years, musicians such as Doucet, Daigrepont, and Zachary Richard were among the cultural heroes who inspired a new wave of recruits, including Steve Riley, Richard LeBoeuf, and Blake Mouton. Many young musicians who came up through the ranks—Robert Jardell, Johnny Sonnier, Terry Huval, Reggie Matte, and Paul Daigle, to name a few—have emerged as the leaders of today's Cajun music. A few who have been willing to take to the interstates, such as Doucet, Zachary Richard, and Wayne Toups, have made names far beyond Louisiana. Others, such as Walter Mouton, have preferred to stick to the parish roads closer to home, emulating earlier musicians like Octa Clark, who never wandered farther than a few hours' drive from his native Judice.

Although women generally have avoided the bandstand, many have helped to preserve Cajun music in subtler ways. Some sang ballads and folksongs to their children. Others played instruments. Prominent Cajun musicians such as Nathan Abshire, Eddie Lejeune, and Don Montoucet reported learning from their mothers and grandmothers at home. And recently a few women musicians, such as Sheryl Cormier and Becky Richard, have emerged, following the lead of Cleoma Falcon, who performed with her husband, Joseph, on the very first recording of Cajun music in 1928. Jane Grosby Vidrine, Ann Allen Savoy, and Sharon Arms Doucet married Cajun musicians (John Vidrine, Marc Savoy, and Michael Doucet) and have joined their husbands in the band.

Steve Riley and Wayne Toups, who both fell in love with Cajun music at an early age, exemplify the two main directions in which contemporary Cajun music seems to be moving. Toups grew up accompanying his parents to Saturday night French dances around his native Crowley. He quit school before his teen years to work in the rice fields, so he missed out on the high-school social scene, steeped in rock and roll, of the sixties and seventies. His brother inspired him to try the accordion, and he quickly excelled, studying the styles of masters such as Iry Lejeune, Lawrence Walker, and Walter Mouton. Toups's father squired him around to the local dance halls to sit in with the bands; finally, Milton Adams gave the young musician a break, lending Wayne his Midnight Playboys Band to back him at a Christmas Day dance in the mid-1970s. Toups soon organized his own Crowley Aces and recorded several local hits with singer Camey Doucet. By the late seventies, however, Toups had become disenchanted because of a lack of interest in his chosen musical form, especially among the young people in the rural areas. He quit playing to work on the oil rigs, ironically just as Cajun music was beginning to hit stride both in Lafayette and on the national festival circuit. Toups came back a few years later, playing the dance halls again. His performance at the 1984 Cajun Music Festival electrified the crowd, and he quickly became a major figure. His highly innovative style has inspired a legion of admirers, young and old. Toups has jacked the musical level up a few notches with complex arrangements and daring new uses of the accordion, making some strict traditionalists nervous, but it is obvious that he has done his homework. He can and still does play acoustic sets in the old style. Despite the purists' fears, Toups's new material is simply a well-placed next step, in the spirit of earlier innovators such as Joseph Falcon, Nathan Abshire, Belton Richard, and Aldus Roger, each of whom changed the course of Cajun music in his day.

Steve Riley grew up in Mamou, a southwestern Louisiana prairie town long famous for its great Cajun musicians. Unlike most of his generation, he was enamored of Cajun music as a child. By the time Riley was five, his grandfather Burke Guillory had already taught him to sing a few Cajun French songs. Guillory also helped his grandson meet the musical heroes who lived in his own neighborhood: it is evident from Riley's music that Dewey Balfa and Marc Savoy were his mentors. Young Steve listened to Cajun music whenever he could, hanging onto the edge of festival stages like a starstruck groupie. He has pushed the accordion to new limits while carefully respecting the traditional style that first interested him. He is also an accomplished fiddler. Less an iconoclast than Toups, Riley creates a sound that is a careful blend of the rich resources available in his band, the Mamou Playboys, which features Kevin Barzas on guitar, David Greely on fiddle, Mike Chapman on drums, and Dewey's daughter Christine Balfa on triangle. Together the band puts a high-gloss shine on old standards, sometimes tinkering with them, reaching for the edge, speeding them up or modulating them to different keys. This is experimental Cajun music, too, but well within what most would consider to be the cultural boundaries.

From its very beginnings, the so-called Louisiana French renaissance suffered from an identity crisis. The word *Cajun* itself, which had been rehabilitated only since the mid-1970s, posed a problem for many, especially in its English pronunciation and connotation. For many upwardly mobile whites, the word essentially meant "poor-white, French-speaking trash." For black Creoles, *Cajun* was the insult used to respond to *nigger*. Yet now the effort to reclaim cultural pride marched under the Cajun banner. One resulting anomaly was that although CODOFIL's Tribute to *Cajun* Music regularly featured black Creole performers, and their rich musical tradition was honored in the detailed descriptions of the groups, the word *Creole* did not appear in the festival's name. In fact, Chairman Domengeaux fought hard to keep black Creole musicians off the annual poster because he claimed their presence on it "would hopelessly confuse the ethnic issue." At the same time, prominent Creole musicians—Clifton Chenier for one—resisted being lumped into the Cajun music category.

In 1980 Domengeaux moved on to other projects, and he discontinued CODOFIL's sponsorship of the Tribute to Cajun Music. Rubber Boots, the team that actually produced the festival each year as part of the larger Festivals Acadiens, renamed it Festival de Musique Acadienne/Cajun Music Festival, found an eager new sponsor in the Lafayette Jaycees, and immediately arranged to have Creole fiddler Canray Fontenot on the poster. A few years later the festival was dedicated to the legendary Creole accordion player, singer, and composer Amédé Ardoin and focused on the important contributions of black Creole musicians to the development of Cajun music. These were steps in the right direction, but the black Creole community rightly continued to resist getting lost in the Cajun fad, insisting on its own identity. As zydeco accordionist Stanley "Buckwheat" Dural explains, "Instead of one culture, what we have here is two. And both of them are good. We have two good things going."

During the 1950s and 1960s, when Cajuns were beginning to develop the foundation for their cultural movement, black Creoles were preoccupied with what they rightly felt was a more pressing issue, civil rights. Although there are still problems in this regard, no one now notices which bathroom or water fountain people use or where they sit in buses and restaurants. With the easing of Jim Crow segregation, black Creoles have become interested in preserving their position in the cultural landscape of south Louisiana. Their French-influenced background continues to distinguish them from their black neighbors elsewhere in the American South. One of the most important cultural expressions of this community, along with Creole cooking, is its music, zydeco. During the 1980s, Creole activists organized their own Zydeco Festival near Plaisance, in one of the cradles of Creole culture. And recently a group called Creole, Inc., has begun to focus on the black Creole side of the Louisiana French story. People who have historically been isolated because they were, as a local saying goes, "too black to be French and too French to be black" are discovering that what makes their culture so complex is also what makes it so rich. The language of zydeco is an important part of this issue. Whereas Cajun musicians seem to feel that a song has to be in French to be genuine, zydeco musicians are freely translating the lyrics of old songs and composing new ones almost exclusively in English.

One problem in contemporary zydeco is, ironically, related to one of its strengths. Clifton Chenier so dominated zydeco music during his lifetime that his death left a huge void. Yet Clifton himself always encouraged others to follow his lead. Clifton's zydeco was culturally located between Houston and New Orleans, between the blues and jazz, the Delta and the Gulf. It was an ideal illustration of anthropologist Nick Spitzer's notion that French Louisiana is actually the northern tip of the West Indies. In the 1950s, Chenier absorbed the influence of rock and roll and rhythm and blues, and succeeded in translating his percussive zydeco sound into modern terms. His group grew to include electric guitars, bass, drums, a saxophone, and a trumpet, as Clifton carefully built what he presciently named the Red Hot Louisiana Band. The group strained the floor joists under most of the area's dance halls during the straight four-hour sets that are common among performers who play in south Louisiana—there is little time for stargazing when folks want to dance.

The principals of the local zydeco scene will tell you that the recipe for success is to make a record and get it played on local radio and jukeboxes. It's not clear whether Clifton had a plan for getting ahead, but he had the goods, and whether you're making better mousetraps or playing hotter accordion, people will beat a path to your door. He regularly played to packed houses. As often happens, however, his recording career was slower to gel. After recording a couple of tunes for Specialty Records in 1955, he drifted from one regional company to another. He finally returned to the national scene in 1964 with Chris Strachwitz's California-based Arhoolie label, for which he made his most memorable recordings. The Arhoolie releases also attracted the attention of young, hip whites in Lafayette, who began visiting some of the black clubs where Chenier played, including the Blue Angel, the Bon Ton Rouley, Slim's Y Ki Ki in Opelousas, and Richard's in Lawtell. The opportunity to hear the master in his own element overcame their nervousness at being the only whites for blocks around. Clifton's growing popularity soon raced right past racial boundaries, and he became a mainstay at un-air-conditioned, mainly white, student hangouts such as Willie Purple's in Lafayette and the legendary Jay's Lounge and Cockpit in Cankton.

Clifton Chenier believed that his hot zydeco sound could also transcend regional and cultural barriers, and he made annual forays to the edges of America. He recorded for numerous labels and was the subject of several documentary films, including Les Blank's *Hot Pepper*. The fears of those who expected Lawrence Welk–style music from his piano accordion were invariably and immediately laid to rest. The musicians with whom Clifton played during those years make up a virtual all-star team of American blues men and women, old and new, ranging from Big Joe Turner to Big Mama Thornton, B. B. King to Johnny Winter, Ray Charles to Elvin Bishop, Lightnin' Hopkins to Gatemouth Brown. Aware of Europe's long fascination with American jazz and blues, Clifton arranged tours of France, England, Germany, Scandinavia, and Switzerland (where he once set the audience at the prestigious Festival du Jazz in Montreux on its ear with a roaring mixture of zydeco, rock, blues, and Glenn Miller tunes).

Despite his success on the road, Clifton never forgot the way home, playing concerts for concert audiences and dances for dancers. He was keenly aware of his status as a cultural hero. In 1971 the "king of zydeco" first delighted audiences by appearing with a wonderfully gaudy rhinestone-studded crown. By the 1975 Tribute to Cajun Music in Lafayette, all the members of the Red Hot Louisiana Band had smaller, prince-sized crowns. Yet the king maintained close ties with his grass-roots constituency on the local zydeco circuit, regularly holding court over Louisiana bandstand rails from Frilot Cove to Promised Land.

Clifton had an uncanny ability to balance tradition and change. He often spoke of the importance of having followed in his father's footsteps before going off on his own. "Where you come from is what you are," he said just after receiving a Grammy for his 1984 album *I'm Here!* "Whatever you are, be that. Don't try to be more than what you are, and you'll always make it. Don't go above your means. What fits you, stick with it, you know. That's what I did. I figured French music fit me and I stayed with it. Rock and roll didn't get me that Grammy. Zydeco got me that Grammy. Maybe that's going to show some of the young ones that's where it's at, right here. People don't know that. It's here. Just got to do something with it, that's all."

After Clifton's death in 1987, scores of pretenders scrambled to claim his crown. No one emerged a clear winner, but in the aftermath several excellent musicians have distinguished themselves, and zydeco fever has swept the country. Rockin' Dopsie and the Twisters and Buckwheat Zydeco were already hot and touring with major-label contracts when Paul Simon and Hank Williams, Jr., recorded with them, sending zydeco to a prominence that even Clifton could not have anticipated. Terrance Simien's career took off when his Mallet Playboys were featured in the popular film *The Big Easy*. C. J. Chenier is now in the driver's seat of his father's Red Hot Louisiana Band, with his foot to the floor. Some zydeco bandleaders, such as Boozoo Chavis, came out of retirement, while others, like the "Toot Toot" man, Rocking Sidney Simien, crossed over from rhythm and blues when zydeco hit the fast lane. And impressive new talents, such as Nathan Williams and Lynn August, and new groups, such as Zydeco Force and the Zydeco Rockers, continue to emerge as zydeco takes its place on the increasingly diverse American popular music stage. The rising leaders in zydeco are thoughtful young performers who have acquired a firm sense of themselves and the tradition they represent. Lynn August has learned songs from the *juré* tradition to perform alongside his full-blown, full-band arrangements, and Buckwheat has a clause in his performance contract that keeps the cultural record straight by preventing the word *Cajun* from being used to promote his music. Musicians such as Delton Brous-

Clifton Chenier, "king" of zydeco, 1975 Tribute to Cajun Music.

sard, Preston Frank, and John Delafose have applied the passage of tradition even more directly, by bringing their children into their bands.

For all the newfound, hard-won success, tensions exist within the zydeco community. Groups interested in preserving the past complain about the fast pace of change. For example, Lawrence Ardoin says that younger crowds find the older style he inherited from his father, Alphonse "Bois-sec" Ardoin, too French. Fiddlers, an important part of early zydeco bands, have been replaced by saxophone or horn players. Preston Frank suggests that the pendulum may be swinging back: he insists that his fiddler, his uncle Carlton Frank, distinguishes the French-oriented, old-time Frank Family Zydeco Band, and that younger crowds are interested in the old stuff as long as it is energized. "Some places you have a demand for a fiddle. That's why we keep one with us. I always did like it. Some people don't, but I always did. And some people want it. You've got a lot of young people involved in this now. They're not too interested in disco or other kinds of music too much anymore. It's strictly zydeco. Sometimes the young people have a different style of zydeco music. Some bands don't play waltzes at all anymore. But we find that people ask us if we know waltzes, too. Even the young people like to dance waltzes sometimes." His children, Keith, Jennifer, and Brad, come from a generation that may once have hidden its interest in zydeco, but now they find that playing in the family band gives them a certain local stardom. Friends notice their performances on the "Zydeco Extravaganza" weekly television program, hear their music on the weekend zydeco radio shows, and see their records in the shops. The kind of social status that for a while was reserved for outsiders is available once again inside the Creole community's own cultural boundaries.

On the other hand, the influence of rhythm and blues, soul and just plain blues is so close and so strong that some zydeco musicians can forget what they are playing and why. When a Danish television crew tried to film a local group a few years ago, the group switched from zydeco to rhythm and blues when the lights went on. The disappointed and unimpressed crew turned off the lights. The musicians had misunderstood what attracted attention to them in the first place. Other groups have a firmer sense of what and why they're playing. Stanley Dural explains the balancing act between achieving popularity and maintaining integrity in the zydeco community, with strong words for those who would compromise themselves and their heritage for money: "I'm going to get on stage tonight. I'm going to kick off my show. If the people like it, I'm going to hang on it for a while. But you can't eat pork chops every day. If it's not right for them, you'd better mix that mosquito up, brother, because something's going to happen. There's no limit to what you can do for an audience. If the audience is happy, then you're happy. You think about the money later. But then, if you're not happy with what you're doing, if the audience is not happy, man, get yourself another job. Some musicians come and take the accordion and it's a damn joke. So you call that just to make a dollar. I love music, but I hate people destroying music, misrepresenting it. That accordion is not just a money-making machine."

Despite the grim predictions of their demise, both Cajun music and zydeco are still alive and even well again. And now that they have regained their footing, they are quite confidently striding toward the future by pathways they determine for themselves despite the fads running rampant today. Both kinds of music are important parts of a budding cultural-tourism-based economy. Their skyrocketing popularity has brought problems as well as opportunities. When asked if he thought it unfortunate that the Cajuns have been "dis-

Nathan Abshire, 1975 Tribute to Cajun Music.

covered," Marc Savoy responded, "What's more unfortunate is that the Cajuns have discovered themselves." He went on to express his fear that the culture could die of "acute cuteness." Indeed, one can now go fishing in a Cajun brand bass boat with Cajun brand crickets for bait and Cajun brand ice in a Cajun brand ice chest to keep the catch cold so that it will be fresh when fried on a Cajun brand outdoor burner. Even outside concerns have jumped (rather awkwardly) on the bandwagon. A Milwaukee brewer marketed a Cajun brand beer laced with cayenne pepper—a concoction no one in south Louisiana ever dreamed of drinking; it died a quick and merciful death. Meanwhile, Creoles are left to wonder what happened to their contribution to the French Louisiana cultural gumbo. McCajun Fries and Cajun Whalers aside, however, I like to think that the Cajun and Creole cultures have revitalized themselves beyond the quick fix.

Cajun music and zydeco have joined Cajun and Creole food as major cultural exports. Displaced Cajuns and Creoles stay in touch. The Cajun Music Festival now gets demo tapes from groups as widely dispersed as the Edinburgh (Scotland) Playboys, who went to work offshore in the North Sea, and the California Cajun Orchestra, who moved to the Bay Area for economic opportunity. Creole musicians such as Queen Ida and Danny Poulard also stay in touch from the West Coast. Some non-Cajun and non-Creole groups and individuals, such as Bayou Seco from New Mexico and Jim McDonald from New York, are opening a new front—and raising new issues of authenticity—by becoming interested in these heretofore quintessentially local music forms and learning to play them. California's Arhoolie Records and Massachusetts' Rounder Records are among the leading producers of Cajun and zydeco recordings, along with Louisiana's own Swallow Records. But even while Cajun and Creole musicians are making inroads on the national and international scenes, the real heart of the music continues to beat in the dance halls and church halls throughout south Louisiana and southeast Texas.

Dewey Balfa delivered a brilliant extemporaneous address on cultural conservation at the 1985 Smithsonian Festival of American Folklife. Invited to the festival as a spokesman for the effort to conserve America's traditional culture, he announced halfway through a forty-five-minute set that up to that point he had been playing traditional songs fifty years old or more. Now, he said, he was going to perform some new songs, songs that he and his brothers had composed just before Rodney and Will died in 1978. He added that he didn't have to turn around to know that he had just made some

people backstage very nervous, since he was there to represent cultural conservation. "But for me," he explained, "cultural conservation doesn't mean freezing culture or preserving it under glass. It means preserving the life of the culture, and if we are successful, then our culture is going to be alive and well and continue to grow. And fifty years or so from now in Louisiana, some young musicians are going to need some songs that are fifty or so years old to play, so my brothers and I made some, and I'm going to play a few of them for you now." Interestingly, his new songs sounded just like his old ones because, as Dewey went on to explain, "they are coming from the same place, through the same process, and they are being played by the same person."

The Lafayette festival, which helped to rejuvenate the Louisiana French music scene in 1974, is still around, keeping in touch with what seems to be important today, following new trends, new developments, and new players. It also still brings together old masters and Young Turks in an ongoing effort to both water the roots and throw light on the new branches. The Festival de Musique Acadienne now has plenty of company. Many other festivals, special concerts, restaurants, dance halls, and radio and television shows in south Louisiana and beyond regularly feature Cajun music and zydeco. For just one example, the Jean Lafitte National Historical Park's Acadian Culture Center features a permanent exhibition on the development of Cajun music and zydeco and presents a weekly interpretive concert and live radio show in the Liberty Theater in Eunice. Offerings such as this give the local population new chances to understand and appreciate their heritage and its music.

Meanwhile, with their growing acceptance and popularity, Louisiana French musicians now perform in places that would once have been considered highly unlikely, from presidential inaugurations to Carnegie Hall, and perhaps most important, in many south Louisiana schools. Yet beneath all the flash and glitter, today's performers are simply doing what Cajun and zydeco musicians have always done: creating new songs and finding new directions for growth, all the while drawing on the deep roots of their traditions. That is how music is made when a culture is alive and well.

Of course, nothing is ever certain. Ongoing cultural and linguistic conservation efforts will affect the future of both traditions. And important questions remain. Is "Jolie Blonde" sung in English still Cajun music? And just what is the dividing line between zydeco and soul? The next generation will have to fight at least as hard as the last to preserve the culture in and beyond themselves. In the words of Dewey Balfa, "A culture is preserved one generation at a time."

Cajun Music
AND Zydeco

Felix Richard, Cankton, Louisiana, 1988.

Dewey Balfa and daughter Christine, Festival de Musique Acadienne, Lafayette, Louisiana, 1990.

Accordion jam session, Ugly Day, Mamou, Louisiana, 1991.

Wayne Toups, Kingfish Beach, Lafayette, 1991.

Dauphine zydeco club, Parks, Louisiana, 1991.

6

Zydeco benefit dance, Immaculate Conception Church, Lebeau, Louisiana, 1991.

Nathan Williams and the Zydeco Cha Chas, Dauphine Club, Parks, 1991.

Germaine Jack, frottoir player, Richard's Club, Lawtell, Louisiana, 1988.

Road sign, Richard's Club, Lawtell, 1991.

Zydeco Force and fan, Hamilton's Place, Lafayette, 1991.

"Rendez Vous des Cajuns" radio broadcast, Liberty Theater, Eunice, Louisiana, 1990.

Fiddler David Greely, Mardi Gras, Mamou, 1990.

Emile and Louis Ancelet, annual family cochon de lait (pig roast), Ossun, Louisiana, 1989.

Dennis McGee, Highway 190 outside Savoy Music Center, Eunice, 1986.

Dennis McGee, USL's honorary dean of Cajun music with, left, Preston Manuel and, right, Sady Courville, half time, Cajun Field, Lafayette, 1982.

Dennis McGee at home with his former pupil Michael Doucet, Eunice, 1989.

Michael Doucet, Lafayette, 1989.

Beausoleil at Mulate's, Breaux Bridge, Louisiana, 1987.

Beausoleil at Great American Music Hall, San Francisco, 1989.

Ardoin Family Band, Weill Recital Hall at Carnegie Hall, New York City, 1990.

Morris Ardoin backstage at Carnegie Hall, 1990.

Alphonse "Bois-sec" Ardoin, at home, Duralde, Louisiana, 1991.

"Bois-sec" Ardoin, Duralde, 1991.

Canray Fontenot with visitors, Vermilionville, Lafayette, 1991.

Canray Fontenot at home, Welsh, Louisiana, 1991.

Young Steve Riley, Festival de Musique Acadienne, Lafayette, 1984.

A young boy watches adult Steve Riley perform, Mamou, 1991.

Steve Riley, Mamou, 1991.

Sign, Cajun Music Festival, Mamou, 1991.

Storm rising, Cajun Riviera Music Festival,
Holly Beach, Louisiana, 1991.

Signs at Zydeco Festival entrance, Plaisance, 1989.

Bébé Carriere at Slim's Y Ki Ki, Opelousas, Louisiana, 1985.

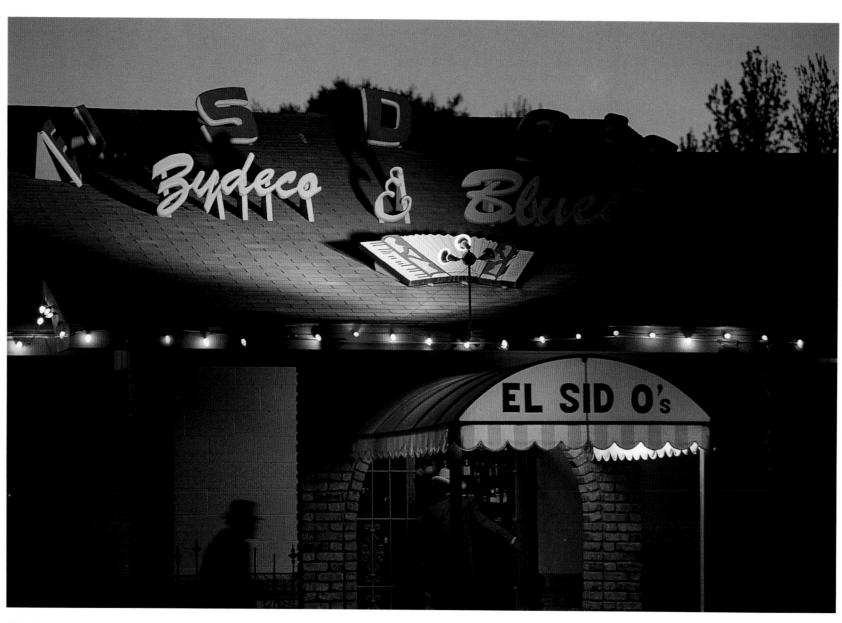

El Sid O's Club, Lafayette, 1991.

Dancing to Zydeco Force, Festival International de Louisiane, Lafayette, 1991.

Willis Prudhomme and Zydeco Express,
Yambilee Jam, Opelousas, 1991.

Sacred Heart Church parish hall, Port Arthur, Texas, 1991.

44

Zydeco dance, Sacred Heart parish hall, Port Arthur, 1991.

Clifton Chenier at home, Lafayette, 1983.

Buckwheat Zydeco at home, Carencro, Louisiana, 1991.

C. J. Chenier at Festival International de Louisiane, Lafayette, 1990.

Aldus Roger at Mulate's, Breaux Bridge, 1991.

Eddie Lejeune, son of Iry Lejeune, at home, Welsh, 1991.

D. L. Menard under a green oak tree, Youngsville, Louisiana, 1987.

D. L. Menard with grandchildren at his chair factory near home, Erath, 1987.

Hamilton's Place, Lafayette, 1991.

Hamilton's Place, Lafayette, 1991.

Ann Goodly with her grandfather at his zydeco club, Papa Paul's, Mamou, 1985.

Ann Goodly at Zydeco Festival, Plaisance, 1990.

Ambrose Sam, Festival International de Louisiane, Lafayette, 1990.

Leon Sam, nephew of Ambrose Sam, Festival International de Louisiane, Lafayette, 1990.

David Rubin, "Dopsie, Jr.," at Zydeco Festival, Plaisance, 1987.

Bruce Daigrepont at Tipitina's, New Orleans, 1988.

John Delafose with Joseph "Slim" and Charles Prudhomme, Richard's Club, Lawtell, 1985.

Doug Kershaw, Lake Arthur, Louisiana, 1989.

Zachary Richard and Wayne Toups, Festival de Musique Acadienne, Lafayette, 1989.

Zachary Richard, Festival de Musique Acadienne, Lafayette, 1986.

Monsoon survivors, Festival de Musique
Acadienne, Lafayette, 1982.

Dancers, Festival de Musique Acadienne, Lafayette, 1989.

Zydeco frottoirs for sale, Festival International de Louisiane, Lafayette, 1991.

La Poussière Cajun dance hall, Breaux Bridge, 1988.

Walter Mouton and the Scott Playboys, La Poussière, Breaux Bridge, 1991.

Bourque's Club, Lewisburg, Louisiana, 1987.

Warning sign, Fred's Lounge, Mamou, 1991.

Fred's Lounge, Mamou, 1991.

Les Bon Temps Dancers, Mardi Gras,
Iota, Louisiana, 1991.

Don Montoucet and the Wandering Aces, Festival de Musique Acadienne, Lafayette, 1983.

Nathan Abshire on accordion, Tribute to Cajun Music, Lafayette, 1977.

Terrance Simien, Montreal Jazz Festival, 1991.

Crowd watching Terrance Simien, Montreal Jazz Festival, 1991.

Nathan Williams, Dauphine Club, Parks, 1991.

Slim's Y Ki Ki, Opelousas, 1985.

Guidry's Friendly Lounge, Lewisburg, 1991.

Guidry's Friendly Lounge, Lewisburg, 1991.

Mother's Day dance, Smiley's Bayou
Club, Erath, Louisiana, 1991.

Dancers, Randol's restaurant, Lafayette, 1988.

Dewey Balfa, family crawfish boil, Basile, Louisiana, 1991.

Barry Ancelet, host, and David Greely at "Rendez Vous des Cajuns" radio broadcast, Eunice, 1991.

Dancing to zydeco version of the "Harlem Shuffle," Hamilton's Place, Lafayette, 1991.

Paul Simon with Terrance Simien and C. J. Chenier, in concert, Lafayette, 1991.

Jeffrey Broussard of Zydeco Force and father Delton Broussard of the Lawtell Playboys, Opelousas, 1991.

Jimmy Sherrill, Kevin Carrier, Chubby Carrier, and father Roy Carrier, Zydeco Festival, Plaisance, 1991.

Zydeco dance after zydeco trail ride, Lake Charles, 1987.

Livonia Meche at La Poussière, Breaux Bridge, 1988.

Musicians' wives, Mother's Day, Smiley's Bayou Club, Erath, 1991.

Jim Soileau reads supermarket ad on radio show, Fred's Lounge, Mamou, 1991.

Ann Savoy (fiddle) with Tina Pilione, Saturday morning jam session, Savoy Music Center, Eunice, 1991.

Cory McCauley, Festival de Musique Acadienne, Lafayette, 1991.

Kevin Barzas, Mamou, 1991.

Sheryl Cormier and the Cajun Sounds,
Holly Beach, 1991.

Children's Mardi Gras, Basile, 1986.

Music wagon, Mardi Gras, Mamou, 1991.

Dennis Israel (accordion) on music wagon,
Mardi Gras, Mamou, 1991.

Lionel Leleux, fiddle maker, with fiddle back, Leleux, Louisiana, 1991.

Lionel Leleux in workshop, Leleux, 1991.

Raymond Himel, zydeco frottoir maker, Champagne's sheet metal shop, Lafayette, 1991.

Marc Savoy, accordion maker, Eunice, 1991.

Marc Savoy with daughter Sarah at home, Eunice, 1983.

Nezpiqué at home, Scott, 1991.

Preston Frank and his Zydeco Family Band at home, Soileau, Louisiana, 1991.

Dancers, Hamilton's Place, Lafayette, 1991.

118

Richard and Anne Baron, last dance, Mulate's, Breaux Bridge, 1988.

After dance, Vermilionville, Lafayette, 1991.